This is a history of:

....

I started this journal on:

....

in the city of:

....

I completed this journal on:

....

in the city of:

....

This journal is especially for:

....

This is my history and it is also your history. I hope
that as you read it, you will be encouraged to
keep a journal so your children can
learn all about you.

for My Child

A Mother's Keepsake Journal

by Linda Kranz

photography by Klaus Kranz

Northland Publishing

MORE JOURNALS BY LINDA KRANZ:

All About Me: A Keepsake Journal for Kids
More About Me: Another Keepsake Journal for Kids
Through My Eyes: A Journal for Teens

☙━◆━❧

The text type was set in Fairfield
The display type was set in Bodoni Antiqua
Designed by Billie Jo Bishop
Edited by Stephanie Bucholz
Printed in Hong Kong

FIRST IMPRESSION, MARCH 1998
Special B.A.F. Printing, January 2000
ISBN 0-87358-633-6

161/100M/1-00

With a smile, for my parents, Jayne and Bill, and
my parents-by-marriage, Anni and Willi. Your love
and encouragement set me on my life path.
I am lucky in so many ways.

And for all Moms:
Instill the belief in your children that they can
do *anything* if they only try.

Introduction

TIME PASSES SO QUICKLY. Often when I speak with friends and we talk about our children, the past, and daily experiences, they say, "Oh, how I wish I had written down these memories. Time just seems to fly by." My answer to them is: "It's never too late to start. There is so much you could write about, I'm sure you could fill a book." They agree, yet they still don't know where to start.

Over the years I have kept journals for both of my children. I fill them with things they have said, their accomplishments, things we did as a family, the cost of gas and groceries, my experiences in the work force, frustrations, triumphs, and the matters of everyday life. In the margins I write quotes that have inspired me and recipes that I have enjoyed making. I have carried these journals with me to doctors' appointments and when I got the oil changed in my car. I have written during breaks and lunchtime at work. When I began to think about creating a journal for others, a friend said, "Model it for us—your friends. Give us a vehicle to do the same thing for our children." So here it is.

This journal will be treasured by your children when it is complete. It will capture memories that they might not be aware of because they were too busy growing up.

A Note About Using This Journal

There are two sections to this journal. The first and larger section, "About Me," has "thought-starters" using "I" as the subject to help inspire you to write about yourself. The second section, "About You," has thought-starters about "you" that are meant to help you think of things to write about your child.

This journal is a place for you to reflect, to dream, and to outline your ideas. I want you to capture, in your own words, your life story and all that is important to you, so that when your child reads it he or she will truly know you.

Be honest and candid in your entries. Choose a question that sparks a memory for you on any particular day. Go in any order you like. Skip around. Give yourself time. Look through old photographs; they always bring back memories. On the pages that say "Write more memories here," you can write thought-starters that are specific to your family. In this way you can further personalize this journal for you and your child.

I suggest dating your responses. This will help your child realize where you were coming from when you wrote them.

Notice the positive reinforcing statements throughout the journal: gentle reminders of things that we know, yet sometimes forget because we get wrapped up in our day-to-day activities. Enjoy them. And put them into action.

Have fun with these questions. Begin your writing *now!*

—LINDA KRANZ

About me

Childhood memories.

Where I was born. First friends that I remember.
Games I played, favorite stories. A time I was scared.
A time I felt proud.

I was born in St. Louis, mo
at St. John's Hospital. This
is the same Hospital you
were born at. I was born
on July 2, 1974. I weighed
6 lb. 7 ounces. I have 2 older
brothers & sisters Doug & Chris but
my youngest sister Jennifer was
who I spent most of my childhood
playing with. Even though we used to
fight alot when we were
younger we became best friend
when we became adults.

Memories of my school days.

The schools I went to. My favorite teachers. Classrooms that I can remember.

Kindergarten and 1st grade I went to Chesterfield elementary school in St. Louis Missouri. Second and third grade my parents tranferred us to Catholic School at Ascension. The summer before fourth grade our family moved to the Country to Potosi missouri. I didn't like living down there because there was nothing to do in the Country, fourth through sixth grade we lived down there. My parents owne a Greenhouse and Florist down there. That Part was fun. When I started Junior High my parents moved us back to Ballwin missouri. Seventh through nineth grade I went to Selvidge Junior High. Tenth through twelveth grade I attended Lafayette Senior High. I never liked school at all until I went away to college at Central Missouri State Univ. in Warrensburgh Missour about 45 min. from Kans City. I had a great time

up there. I was in a
Sorority Sigma Kappa.
I spent three years
up there but I wasn't
a very good student. I
guess I had a little too
much fun. I decided
college wasn't for me
so I came back home and got a job as
a file clerk at a law firm. It was a good
job and it gave me good experience in an
office setting.

My favorite subject.

My saddest memory.

My happiest memory.

Fond memories of my parents when I was growing up.

Our daily routine. What we would talk about.
How we shared feelings.

I had great Parents. They Gave us pretty much anything we wanted without spoiling us. My mom & I clashed alot the older I got. I think because we were alot alike. We didn't become good friends until you were born. I think then I appreciated her more. My Father and I were always close, I was always daddy's little girl. He always protected me and he always supported me through everything that happened in my life.

Now that I'm ___ years old,

these are the things I've learned about life, love, friends, family.
(Keep adding to this list.)

Places I have lived.

About the city or town I live in now. How I came to live here. The population. Changes I have seen in the time I have lived here. Interesting things close by.

Memories of houses I have lived in.

The yards. About our house now. What room I like the best, and why.
The things I like about our neighborhood.

About your father.

Where he was born. His family. His memories of school.

His first job. Jobs he has had over the years. How he feels about his profession. If he could change jobs right now, he would:

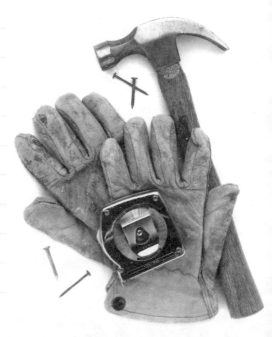

Dinnertime:

The meals we usually eat. Topics we discuss.

My average weekday.

How it starts, develops, and ends. Does it change as the seasons change?

The weekend. How it starts, develops, and ends.

What I like to do on the weekend.

Favorite family recipes.

**Things
I collect.**

*How I came to collect them and why I like them. Where I
have found some of my favorites. How long I've been collecting them.*

The weather.

What time of year I like best. Dangerous weather I have seen.
Beautiful sunsets, starry nights.

My favorite holiday when I was growing up.

*The memories that come to mind. My favorite holiday now that I'm grown.
Our family traditions that go with it.*

My thoughts about pets.

Pets I had as a child.

Their names. My memories of them.

Write more memories here.

Encourage laughter.

Read to your children.

Hugs go a long way
when words don't fit.

Remember to compliment
your children every chance you get.

My memories about how I learned to drive.

What I have learned over the years about driving. About cars.

My first car. My favorite car.

Memories of my first Mother's Day.

My feelings. Other Mother's Days that I especially remember.

The emotions I felt when I discovered we
were going to have a child.

The first people we told.

My thoughts and feelings when I saw you for the first time.

What I remember about that day.

How we decided on your name.

How prices have changed over the years.

The cost of a doctor's visit. The weekly grocery bill for our family.
The price of gas. Utility bills. House payments.

The kind of music played in our house when I was young.

The kind of music I enjoy listening to now.

My first job.

What it was like. Other jobs I have had. My favorite job. The ups and the downs of working. Suggestions about choosing a career.

Friends.

How we met. How we have managed to stay in

touch over the years.

What it means to be a friend.

What I have done differently with my own family compared
to what my parents did when they raised me.

Things I love.

(Keep adding to this list.)

What I think the future will be like.

The changes I would like to see. I hope that in your lifetime . . .

How I met your father.

What interested me in him. How old we were. How long we dated.
Our favorite song. What I know now about him that I didn't know on our wedding day.

Special memories of your father and me.

We see eye to eye on some matters,
but on others we do not.

Memories of our wedding day.

Where we were married. The people who attended. Those who couldn't come that we truly missed. Where we went on our honeymoon and what it was like.

If I had to describe a few of my happiest memories,
these are the ones I would think of right away:

Vacations I remember going on

as a child and through the years. Good ones and bad.

If I could change three things about myself, they would be . . .

1)

2)

3)

Things I would do differently if I were to have another child.

Things I would relax about. Things I would notice more.

Ways your father has surprised me over the years. Ways I have surprised him.

Stand-out surprises I remember.

Places I have visited that I want to tell you about.

My memories of those places and what I liked or disliked about them. Thoughts on traveling.

Favorite foods.

How my tastes have changed since I was young.
My favorite snacks, desserts, drinks . . .

My favorite movies.

Why I watch them over and over.

An important lesson or two that I have learned.

Write more memories here.

Point out beautiful things
to your children so they will learn
to look for good things on their own.

Encourage independence and
uniqueness in your children.

Choose your words carefully; they can crush an
enthusiastic spirit faster then you realize.

Encourage; don't criticize.

My wish list.

Things that I don't necessarily need, but would enjoy having.
(Keep adding to the list. When each wish is realized, star it and add the date.)

Things I've done that have taken me out of my comfort zone.

How it felt to take risks. How those things turned out.

How I feel about my name.

The story behind how my parents chose my name. Other names I like.

Toys I remember

from my childhood.

Toys I still have.

If I could *travel* anywhere in the world it would be . . .

Why I would choose this place.

If I could *live* anywhere I wanted,

I would choose . . .

Never be too busy to stop
and listen to your child.

When was the last time you said "I love you"
to your children? Tell them often, so they will
know that it is true.

Involve your child in
decision making.
Explain your decisions.

If someone gave me a million dollars,

no strings attached, this is what I would do.

If I had to name a few things my parents taught me they would be . . .

....

....

....

....

....

....

....

....

....

....

....

I hope that, when my children are grown, they will say they learned this from me:

....

....

....

....

....

....

....

....

....

....

....

....

Trace around your hand and write the date. Use colored pencils to make your silhouette unique. Your child will cherish this page and want to place his or her hand on yours.

How my parents made/make a living.

Memories of their jobs.

When I am gone I want to be remembered this way . . .

If I had to describe the most challenging part of being a parent, I would say . . .

....

....

....

....

....

....

....

....

....

If I had to describe the most rewarding

     part of being a parent, I would say . . .

....

....

....

....

....

....

....

....

....

Some of my favorite books

and the reasons they mean so much to me.

Write more memories here.

Encourage your children to write thank-you notes
when they receive gifts.

Set aside time just for you and your children to share.
They will love the interaction and you will be
absorbed by their fresh view of life.

Every child needs his or her own space. Honor
it. Allow it. Encourage it. Knock before entering
your child's room.

Some of the happiest memories of my grandparents.

People I admire and why.

Some things I have done that I'm proud of.

Write more memories here.

Let your children express themselves in their own way.
Don't interrupt. Be patient.

Be understanding.

Studies are essential, but so are friendship
and family time. Teach your children how
to balance these things.

Some thoughts on relationships:

friends, family, children. How relationships change.

My favorite . . .

Flowers. Smell. Sound. Color. Why these are my favorites.

How technology has changed since I was young.

When I was young, more than anything else I used to wish for . . .

Memories of my sisters and brothers.

How many years between us. How we got along when we were young.
How we get along now. How we're different from each other. How we're the same.
Traits and habits we inherited from our parents.

How I like to dress.

Trends I've seen come and go. Trends that are coming back.

My description of success,

and some examples I have seen.

Goals I have achieved

and ones I'm working on now.

What part of the day I like best, and why.

What I like to daydream about.

Housework.

How we as a family share the house chores. Shortcuts I have learned.

The best thing about getting older. The worst thing.

When I retire, I would like to . . .

A list of things I want to do before I can't do them anymore.

If I were to consider all the birthdays that I have celebrated,

these are the ones that stand out in my memory:

Sacrifices my parents made for me when I was growing up

that I would like to thank them for.

A person in my family history that I would have liked to have a conversation with is:

I would like to know:

The most well-known person I have ever met is . . .

How I met this person, and what I remember most about the meeting.

Autographs

Some pieces of advice that I have received

from family and friends that I'm glad I took to heart.

My talents and hobbies.

How I have developed them over the years. What got me started.

When I think about my dad these words and memories come to mind.

(List at least five to ten words.)

When I think about my mom these words and memories come to mind.

(List at least five to ten words.)

Some of the things I see in my parents that I also see in myself.

First impressions aren't always what they seem.

*These are instances when I was surprised about a person or a situation,
and instances when my first instinct was right.*

Thinking back to how I behaved when I was a teenager.

How my parents handled my many moods.

Things that I am thankful for.

Write more memories here.

Your children watch you so closely. They watch how you react to every situation.

Your expressions mirror your feelings. By watching you they learn how to love.

Given the right tools early in life, children will be well equipped for life and will eventually share those tools with their own children.
They will remember.

About you

Things you have said

that touched me or made me laugh.

Write more memories here.

Save your child's special drawings and school
        work papers. Your children will love to see them
when they have children of their own.

The dishes and housework can wait while
you take an evening walk together with
your child. Enjoy it!

            Remember back to your own childhood
from time to time. This will help
            you see from your child's eyes where he
or she is coming from.

You showed your independence by . . .

What made you a special child.

Some of your best qualities.

On your first day of school I felt . . .

Special teachers you had that made a difference in your life.

How you took to school. Struggles and triumphs.

Your favorite things about school.

Your favorite toys.

Toys you could not part with. Where those toys are now.

Your fears.

How your father and I dealt with them.

Occasions when you were upset or angry about something.

What I did to help.

Things you did that made me proud.

Books you loved through the years.

Presents you made for me over the years.

Siblings.

Ways you would interact.

Or thoughts on being an only child.

Write more memories here.

Take your children to the library and teach them
how to find books that interest them. Go to
the library regularly.

Having children makes you appreciate your own
mother even more. When your patience is
wearing thin, remember that your children
will one day be thankful for everything
you've done for them.

There will come a time when your children
will have to try things on their own. Step aside
and trust that they will be fine. Let go.

The little ways you showed me that you loved me.

When you were sick.

How we made it through those times.

Times when I surprised you.

Your reactions.

Write more memories here.

"If only I had more time I would . . ."
When you catch yourself saying this,
reevaluate your priorities and make time for the
most important aspects of your life.

Don't compare your children to each other.
Realize they won't be the same when it comes
to studies, personality, and outlook on life.
Let them be themselves.

Get to know your child's teacher. Find ways to
be involved in the classroom, such as speaking to
the students about your job, hobbies, and interests.

When I think back to some of your "firsts" these things come to mind:

Statements that you have made with bold honesty.

These words I haven't forgotten.

Things you have said over the years

that weren't quite grammatically correct, but were distinctly "you."

"I'm gonna catch ammonia."

"I'm digging a drench."

"I'm following
their funtprints."

Your room.

How you liked to decorate it.

Best friends and imaginary friends when you were young.

Ways I found to be involved in your school experience.

Your birthdays.

How we celebrated them. Those that I particularly remember.

Watch your children play and interact
with friends
and while they sleep. Remember
these carefree days.

Teach your children how to
take care of their rooms, to cook, to be
responsible. Teach them things they will need to
know when they are on their own
and they will flourish.

Pets.

What they have meant

to you over the years.

Pets we have now.

If I had to write down ten words that describe you, they would be:

1)

2)

3)

4)

5)

6)

7)

8)

9)

0)

What you liked to do in the summer.

Write more memories here.

Take lots of photos.
Your children will grow up so fast!

Brighten your child's day with a note
tucked inside a backpack or lunch bag.

Teach your children kindness.

About the Author

LINDA KRANZ began writing as a teenager. A
locking diary given to her on her thirteenth
birthday was the vehicle that encouraged her to
take to the page. Growing up in a military family
and moving around a lot gave Linda plenty to write
about.

Later, Linda passed her fondness for journaling
on to her daughter, whose interest in keeping her
own journal inspired Linda to write *All About Me: A
Keepsake Journal for Kids,* also from Northland
Publishing.

Linda lives with her husband, Klaus, daughter
Jessica, and son Nikolaus in the mountains of
Flagstaff, Arizona.